The United States National Climate Assessment

NCA Report Series, Volume 2

STRATEGIC PLANNING WORKSHOP

February 24-25, 2010
Chicago, Illinois

United States Global Change Research Program
National Climate Assessment

NCA Report Series, Volume 2: Strategic Planning Workshop

NCA Report Series

The NCA Report Series summarizes regional, sectoral, and process-related workshops and discussions being held as a part of the Third National Climate Assessment (NCA) process.

The first regional and strategic guidance workshops to contribute to the 2013 NCA were held in Chicago in February 2010. Volumes 1 and 2 of the NCA Report Series summarize the discussions and outcomes of these workshops. A list of planned and completed reports in the NCA Report Series can be found online at http://globalchange.gov/what-we-do/assessment.

CONTENTS

CONTENTS

Photo Courtesy of NASA

Overview of the Workshop

The purpose of this meeting was to get input on developing the strategic plan for the next National Climate Assessment, including (1) Preliminary mission, goals, principles, and structure (components) of the National Assessment; (2) Identifying key partners and engagement strategies; (3) Suggestions for governance structure (administration, technical, financial); (4) Timeline and milestones for National Assessment and related outputs; (5) Topics: regions, sectors, scenarios?; and (6) Desired outcomes.

The majority of the roughly 70 participants in this meeting had been involved in assessments and climate-related decision processes in the past, or had evaluated or managed similar processes. They represented a wide range of sectors, regions, government agencies and universities. Many of the participants in this meeting also attended the "Midwest Regional Workshop," held just prior to this meeting, on February 22-24 in Chicago. A number of comments and observations from that workshop served as inputs to the discussions held at this meeting. For more information about the Midwest Regional Workshop and its outcomes, please see the report.[1]

The format of this workshop included both plenary sessions and facilitated breakout sessions. All sessions were recorded and highlights reported back for plenary wrap-up sessions. The agenda is attached as Appendix A, and the Participant List is Appendix B.

Ahead of the meeting, participants were given a preliminary draft of the mission, goals, and principles for the National Assessment (Box 1). A number of themes that arose during the preliminary discussion of these are highlighted below. The discussion of these issues continued to evolve throughout the meeting, especially as the participants began to move toward practical questions related to implementing the Assessment process; these conversations are captured in subsequent portions of the report, especially under "Key Messages Wrap-up: Approaches to National Climate Assessment" and "Building an Enduring Assessment Structure."

---

[1] National Research Council. 2009. Restructuring Federal Climate Research to Meet the Challenges of Climate Change. Washington, DC: The National Academies Press. http://www.nap.edu/catalog.php?record_id=12595.

Defining the Federal Context for the Assessment

Because there are multiple ongoing and recently initiated assessment, adaptation and climate service efforts inside and outside the Federal Government, there is a strong need to identify the boundaries between what the National Assessment is per se, and other important activities such as:

- The NOAA Climate Service (and associated climate service activities in other agencies) focused on supporting climate-related decisions

- The development of the National Adaptation Strategy, with leadership assigned to Council on Environmental Quality (CEQ), Office of Science and Technology Policy (OSTP) and NOAA

- The DOI Regional Climate Change Response Centers and Landscape Conservation Cooperatives, which are partnerships focused on regional resource management issues

- Ongoing assessment and adaptation activities within multiple agencies, including EPA, NOAA, USDA, multiple DOI agencies and others

- Ongoing assessment activities within states, sectors and NGOs

Perhaps the most challenging and important of the coordination efforts is defining the relationship of the Assessment and all of the activities above to the U.S. Global Change Research Program's science activities. In light of the discussions of relevance and the desire to inform adaptation and mitigation choices around the country, it was suggested that other federal departments and agencies that may not currently be represented in the USGCRP may need to be engaged.

The need for interagency coordination and a clear articulation of the boundaries of these activities was a prominent theme in the discussion. Multiple observers noted that none of this will be possible without strong leadership support within OSTP, some reorganization and reprioritization of resources at USGCRP and a cooperative relationship between CEQ, USGCRP and OSTP. There is significant potential for confusion, redundancy, or competition between agencies, especially at the regional level,

with DOI and NOAA both initiating regional climate center activities. There is a need for a clear strategic framing of the Assessment process that is integrated in the broader, evolving USGCRP context (adaptation, services, CCSP, CCTP), but also realistic goals consistent with users' and providers' needs and capacities, and a detailed implementation plan. At the meeting, a diagram showing the intersection of the science, adaptation and mitigation efforts (Figure 1) was widely supported, but viewed as just one part of the puzzle.

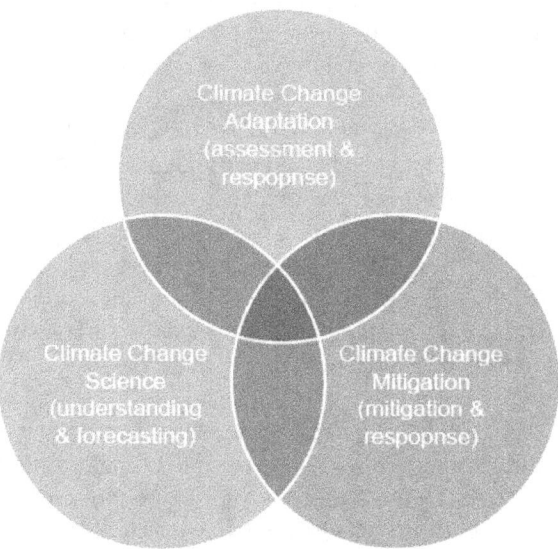

Figure 1. Conceptual framework for organization of the Federal climate enterprise.

Defining the Audience
There are multiple audiences for the Assessment, and different kinds of processes and products can be developed to respond to the needs of specific priority groups and stakeholders. Clear articulation of the goals of the Assessment, as well as communication of expectations and limitations on capacity to deliver is critical, as is having a strong communications strategy that is ingrained in the fabric of the Assessment. It is important not to over-promise. Products should be designed for impact, whether they are designed for the media, federal agencies, policymakers, individual decision-makers, or regional interest groups. Both of the previous sets of National Assessment activities fell short in the outcomes department, in part because there was not an effective strategy for follow through and engagement of important audiences such as decision-makers whose responsibilities include resources and infrastructure likely to be impacted by climate change. Metrics of success need to provide a clear line of sight between

the investment in the Assessment and improvements in social and environmental welfare.

There was concern expressed about identifying stakeholders more broadly and more carefully than has been done in the past. Working closely with opinion leaders in regions and sectors to define the key questions and the important players can result in a much more informed approach to engagement. Working to "co-produce" products with partners in the private sector, governments at all levels, NGOs, academia and educators should help ensure both connections to key stakeholders and their constituents in any given region or sector and the relevance and usefulness of assessment products. Non-traditional stakeholder groups, including young and older people, should be included. Care should be taken not to impose federal solutions on local decision-makers –a national framework is needed, but in many cases entities need more "discussion support" (e.g., how to frame the problem and identify potential solutions) than "decision support" (which may appear to be too prescriptive or may be too theoretical for real world applications).

It was noted that federal agencies, government scientists and Congress also need to use information produced by the Assessment. It is important not to define the term stakeholder too narrowly. Stakeholders are people who have a stake in the issue, and that turns out to be a very large group with a vast array of interests and needs.

Framing the Assessment: Mission, Goals, and Principles for the National Climate Assessment

Prior to the meeting, participants were provided with a preliminary draft of the mission, goals, and principles for the National Assessment (Box 1). A number of themes that arose during the preliminary discussion of these are highlighted below. The discussion continued to evolve throughout the meeting, especially as the participants began to move toward practical questions related to implementing the Assessment process; these conversations are captured in subsequent portions of the report, especially under "Understanding the Alternatives: Approaches to National Climate Assessment" and "Building an Enduring Assessment Structure."

Box 1: Preliminary Mission, Goals, and Principles for the National Climate Assessment

Mission for the National Assessment
The Assessment should support both adaptation and mitigation efforts, including evaluations of interactions between these efforts; establish a broad vision that redefines the Assessment process to explicitly focus on decision support; and build sustained, collaborative relationships between federal agencies and the private and public sectors.

Goals for the National Assessment
1. Timely completion of a report to Congress, responsive to the requirements of the Global Change Research Act (Section 106) (see Box 2).
2. Make the best use of learning from prior Assessments (based on findings of the National Research Council 2007 report, *Analysis of Global Change Assessments: Lessons Learned*) (see Box 3).
3. Develop a sustained capacity to assess impacts, vulnerability, and adaptation and mitigation needs.

Principles for the National Assessment
1. Maximize engagement of federal agencies.
2. Maximize engagement of stakeholders and lasting partnerships outside of the Federal Government, including input and feedback for impacts, mitigation, and adaptation analyses.
3. Prioritize information that helps minimize risk associated with climate change impacts; seek equitable approaches to adaptation and mitigation that protects the most vulnerable regions, ecosystems, populations, and systems (e.g., transportation, energy, etc.).
4. Ensure a sustainable process that supports science, adaptation, climate services, and mitigation efforts, as appropriate.
5. Efficiently coordinate efforts across regions and sectors at multiple scales.
6. Ensure an adaptive approach that responds to new information over time.
7. Include consideration of economic implications of both action and inaction in responding to climate impacts.

Adaptation and Mitigation are Central Themes

From the beginning, the U.S. Global Change Research Act (adopted in 1990) anticipated that the associated climate science investments would support societal outcomes (Box 2). Despite the fact that this mandate has existed for 20 years, the importance of directing the science investments towards decision support has only recently become a priority. It is now recognized as a core component of USGCRP

Box 2: Requirements Related to the National Climate Assessment

Global Change Research Act of 1990, Public Law 101-606, § 106 Scientific Assessment

On a periodic basis (not less frequently than every 4 years), the Council, through the Committee, shall prepare and submit to the President and the Congress an assessment which --

1. integrates, evaluates, and interprets the findings of the Program and discusses the scientific uncertainties associated with such findings;
2. analyzes the effects of global change on the natural environment, agriculture, energy production and use, land and water resources, transportation, human health and welfare, human social systems, and biological diversity; and
3. analyzes current trends in global change, both human- induced and natural, and projects major trends for the subsequent 25 to 100 years.

activity, so this Assessment must support adaptation and mitigation decisions. While past assessments have focused primarily on providing an overview of the impacts of climate change in the United States, the next-generation assessment process must be constructed in such a way that it provides the science and information that the public needs in order to respond to climate change – it must be focused on solutions.

Assessment is Both a Process and a Set of Products

Although the Global Change Research Act sets forth a four-year cycle for providing an assessment document, meeting only this standard would not satisfy the spirit of the requirement. The Assessment should help connect the physical, biological, and social dimensions of climate change and response – it is simultaneously a product, a social communication tool, and a distributed decision support system. Over time, such an assessment process can evolve as it builds trust among stakeholders, expands its scope of inquiry, and is able to address problems that are at a finer scale or have multiple dimensions.

There was a strong consensus among the participants that there is a need for a continuing, sustained assessment process and a well-coordinated set of assessment activities to meet statutory, programmatic, scientific, and societal needs and requirements. Clearly there is a need to produce a "National Assessment" report within the four year time frame required by the GCRA, but it is possible to meet

both the letter of the law and the spirit of the law if the process itself becomes a primary focus. A continuing assessment effort would have the potential to be much more useful in increasing understanding of the state of the science, promoting environmental stewardship, protecting life and property, and reducing vulnerability to the impacts of climate change. Further, the Assessment could be less a "science report" per se and more focused on the success of the process of building human and institutional adaptive capacity in supporting adaptation and mitigation decisions (as well as how they interact), and helping to manage risks and opportunities related to climate change (as suggested by the 2009 NRC report *Restructuring Federal Climate Research* [2]).

Stakeholders are Critical

A poll of participants in the First National Assessment gave the process an average grade of a C+ (though perceptions of the success of the activity varied widely depending on whether the evaluation was done by those "inside" *vs.* "outside" the production team). In order to improve upon this grade, the new process must empower stakeholders inside and outside the government and create a network that persists through time; that is, it must truly be a process that provides stakeholders with ongoing support and access to climate science and information. Right now, many external stakeholders do not feel that federal climate efforts have been adequately responsive to their needs. Engagement with stakeholders is also necessary to ensure that the Assessment is useful, as it is the needs of stakeholders that should ultimately drive the questions and goals of the process (including through "co-production of knowledge" or "participatory research," activities which should be explored as a part of the Assessment process). Because stakeholders are critical to the process, we must think carefully about what the term "stakeholder" actually means and how to be strategic in engaging stakeholders so that an increasing number of participants will benefit from the interactions.

To the degree that regional and sectoral assessment meetings will be held, there is a need to do significant homework on the ground in the regions to identify key issues, opinion leaders and stakeholders prior to having the meeting. It was suggested that we refer to the outcomes of the 22 USGCRP listening sessions that were held in 2007-2009, since that

---

[2] National Research Council. 2009. Restructuring Federal Climate Research to Meet the Challenges of Climate Change. Washington, DC: The National Academies Press. http://www.nap.edu/catalog.php?record id=12595.

effort did capture the perspective of a large number of different kinds of stakeholders.[3]

Need for More Science Translation Capacity Across Agencies and Stakeholders

There is a wealth of information and capacity for assessment (e.g., observations, models, process studies, decision tools, subject matter experts) within federal agencies, but to actually support decisions the information must be made available in ways that stakeholders are able to access and understand. Individual stakeholders and groups of stakeholders have different capabilities to make use of information and capacity (e.g., water managers seem to be fairly technically advanced), and the Assessment process must be able to adjust for these variations. A major focus of the Assessment effort should be on connecting information users with information providers and on ensuring that the appropriate translators are available to work across these groups.

The Assessment should support existing as well as new "boundary spanning" capacity of "translators" between the scientific and policy/management communities, and validation of these activities through resourcing, engagements, and statements of support. Educators and universities can help support the Assessment process and outcomes and engage the academic community and students in building components of the Assessment. More capacity is needed for translation of climate science for specific, sectoral and regional audiences; effective and strategic climate communications; stakeholder identification and engagement; and certain kinds of integrated social science activities within and outside the federal agencies. For example, it was noted that economic considerations are a critical part of decision-making in the real world, yet the ability to assess the economic implications of alternative adaptation or mitigation decisions is almost completely absent within the climate community. Clearly there is a need to build the capacity to do these things.

Focus on Outcomes

There was significant discussion of using metrics other than producing reports that are timely and credible. Outcomes can also be measured in terms of informing policy and improving adaptation and mitigation decisions, building adaptive capacity, transitioning research results into operational use,

enhancing public understanding of climate issues, etc. This type of metric may require new kinds of monitoring, but given the major concerns about the potential implications of climate change, real-world outcomes are important and desirable

Balancing "Scholarly" with "Relevant"

The information sources for the Assessment must include scholarly documents meant to inform policy that are based on published, peer reviewed literature, but these cannot be the only sources. There are a number of non-peer reviewed sources (i.e., "grey literature") that can provide valuable insights and inputs to the Assessment process as well. In some cases, participants in the Assessment will need to submit observed data, collected in a rigorous and well-documented manner that is essential to vulnerability assessment, for example – and yet might never be included in a peer reviewed article. The perception that high quality research is not done in applied contexts is inappropriate here - it is possible to do excellent, rigorous science in support of stakeholder needs.

There are also timing issues relative to peer review, for example, in cases where models and scenarios are just now being developed, there may not be time to go through a full peer review and publication process before these inputs are needed for the Assessment products. Therefore, guidance up front is needed about how to document assessment processes and data to ensure sufficient rigor. All sources should be clearly documented and publicly available so that readers can locate the primary source materials, whether peer reviewed or grey literature. Regardless of how the author teams are selected and the set of products defined, it is essential that the process be transparent and that it begin soon.

[3] A description of the listening sessions and summaries from each of the sessions is available from http://www.globalchange.gov/about/strategic-plan-2003/listening-sessions.

Timing

Given limited resources and the expectation that the next Assessment will include a strong focus on both adaptation and mitigation, in addition to impacts of climate change, the products may need to be staged in such a way that they are able to draw upon previous findings, similar to what is being planned for IPCC's Fifth Assessment Report process. There must also be formal interactions amongst the author teams, across both regions and sectors. Using a staged process can also help build trust and support for the Assessment, as products are iteratively delivered, evaluated, and revised; this may be especially helpful and important for helping to weather the transition between leadership at a variety of scales (e.g., national, state, and local governments; university administrations; NGOs; and private industry).

It will be critical to build the timeline consistent with assessment objectives, the state of the underlying knowledge base, the resources available, and the needs of decision makers. There was discussion about whether or not we should take the time between now and June of 2013 to develop the first of the "new Assessment" reports, or whether it is more advantageous to get a product that meets the GCRA requirements out within two years to avoid the problems associated with having the document in review during a transition between administrations. Given the recommendations above to develop a variety of projects and products over time, many of them could be scheduled to cross the boundary between administrations in hopes of demonstrating the potential to have a continuing, sustained process. The pros and cons of alternative timing approaches need to be evaluated.

Financial Issues

Unless resource availability issues are clarified in the near term, development of the National Assessment will be very constrained. As per the 2007 NRC report, *Analysis of Global Change Assessments*[4], "it is necessary to have adequate funding that is both commensurate with the mandate and effectively managed to ensure an efficient Assessment process." There are current resources earmarked for assessment services within NOAA and a commitment within DOI to support the National Climate Assessment, but decision-making associated with these funds is entirely within the purview of the agencies

involved. EPA and USDA have important ongoing assessment activities. There is the potential to deploy NSF funding in support of Assessment activities, and there are current solicitations that are topically connected. NASA and DOE have indicated the potential to provide support, though mechanisms for doing so are not yet clear. There is a need to engage multiple non-USGCRP agencies, but financial and other roles for agencies need to be identified.

There is a small, shared budget across the 13 USGCRP agencies that is focused on investments that are of mutual interest (including supporting the coordination office of USGCRP), and it appears that the National Climate Assessment central coordination activities could be supported (at least partially) in this way. The magnitude of the overall investment in the Assessment, even a highly constrained version, will far exceed the current shared budget by at least one order of magnitude. As mentioned above, the scale of the Assessment will depend in large part on what resources are available.

A Nested Matrix Approach

Not every issue can be covered equally by the Assessment – the issues of importance vary between regions, the information needed to study a particular issue may not be available at an appropriate scale (or available at all), and there are too many issues to cover with any sort of depth given limited resources. Therefore, the Assessment process should follow a nested approach, in which issues are examined in the places and times that make the most sense in the context of a risk-based prioritization scheme. These focused evaluations can serve as exemplars and test beds upon which to build future rounds of assessment and investigation.

These nested investigations should be pursued within a broad-scale, ongoing monitoring, observations and assessment process that continually updates information about risk, trends, vulnerability, thresholds, *etc.*, using consistent methods over time. In addition to providing input on rates of change and impacts, this "risk matrix" would help ensure that federal investments in science are focused on areas of high priority from a national perspective.

The NRC's *Analysis of Global Change Assessments* provides a recommendation that the National Assessment use this "nested matrix" approach rather than trying to address issues across the country at multiple scales. The actual language in that report recommends "using analysis of large-scale trends

---

[4] National research Council. 2007. Analysis of Global Change Assessments: Lessons Learned. Washington, DC: The National Academies Press. http://www.nap.edu/catalog.php?record_id=11868.

and identification of priority issues as the context for focused, smaller-scale impacts and response assessments at the regional or local level."

Case studies could provide examples of the kinds of information needs and decision support that are needed in a place-based context. There would be an ongoing effort to prioritize individual research investments over time, with outcomes measured in terms of improvements in key indicators of interest to stakeholders, such as a reduction in risk of damage due to sea level rise and storm surges, or improvements in the use of climate forecasts to manage water supplies in reservoirs. Thus, research and assessment could be designed at the scale of decisions and issues rather than being limited to official multi-state regions based on boundaries that may not be relevant to the issues at hand. For example, there can be sectoral cross-cutting issues such as coastal, cities, and industry sectors (construction, manufacturing) and levels of government (e.g., mayors, state officials, tribal leaders) and national security/international issues. It will be important to build on ongoing efforts at various scales and let the decisions (or questions) drive the process. One way to significantly reduce the engagement support requirements is through partnerships with existing networks and associations, e.g., Council of Mayors, Water Utility Climate Alliance, etc.).

The nested approach also allows for sharing of capacity across regions and sectors, and would promote the establishment of a coordinated national network of regionally or sectorally-based partnerships. The development of a virtual clearinghouse and the use of new kinds of information technologies would facilitate access to information and enhance information sharing. The "cyber-support" of the Assessment is an enormous challenge that needs to be linked to existing data collection centers that already exist inside and outside of the federal government.

Assessment as an Integrator
There is significant federal, state, and local attention to adaptation issues and the number of initiatives and projects can be overwhelming. The Assessment process can serve to integrate these various efforts by serving as a common information platform, coordinating with them or even drawing them into the tent of National Assessment. Bringing together these various research, observation and assessment streams and providing a coordinated overview or access point will be tremendously important, as people will not read an entire stack of documents (or even one very fat document). Many stakeholders will be looking to the National Assessment to provide a sense of coherence from the midst seeming chaos. A map or vision of how all the different federal pieces fit together must be developed quickly so that stakeholders are able to engage in meaningful ways.

An Inclusive Vision
Rather than directly supporting decision-making, the Assessment can be viewed as a convener of interests at different scales and a mechanism to bring parties who might not otherwise engage with each other to the table. Another view would be the Assessment as "connective tissue" between other activities such as a national adaptation program, the climate change technology program, and components of climate services. In any of these options the Assessment should focus on identifying the different interests of agencies and stakeholders and trying to forge a collaborative path forward.

Shared Ownership
Significant components of the Assessment activity need to be "co-owned" or at least "co-produced" within the public and private sectors and universities across the U.S. If there is significant non-federal engagement, the process is much more likely to survive changes in administrations. Further, it is likely that external partners have funding, data and staff resources that if properly coordinated can become integral to the overall effort. Finally, relevance to stakeholders is virtually ensured if they are willing to help build the products and services.

The Perfect Should not be the Enemy of the Good
We need to acknowledge that this is a difficult assignment and that we will make mistakes. Furthermore, there are so many different perspectives on what the priorities and approach should be to building the Assessment that it will be easy to criticize. As we have seen in past evaluations of U.S. climate assessments, it is easy to find fault in spite of good intentions and hard work, and the very limited resources that were available. It is important to have a positive outlook and focus on learning from our mistakes.

New Topics for Assessment
A number of sectors and issues not evaluated in previous assessments should be addressed as a part of this new process. These include:
- Observed changes
- Uncertainty

- Tipping points and thresholds
- Adaptation
- Environmental justice
- National security
- Migration
- Island trust holdings

The participants also had an opportunity to review lessons learned from previous assessments and reports, including those of the National Academies. Important advice from the Academies is outlined in Box 3.

Box 3: Essential Elements of Effective Assessments
National Research Council, 2007. *Analysis of Global Change Assessments: Lessons Learned.* National Academies Press: Washington, DC. http://books.nap.edu/catalog.php?record_id=11868.

1. A clear strategic framing of the Assessment process, including a well-articulated mandate, realistic goals consistent with the needs of decision makers, and a detailed implementation plan.
2. Adequate funding that is both commensurate with the mandate and effectively managed to ensure an efficient assessment process.
3. A balance between the benefits of a particular assessment and the opportunity costs (e.g., commitments of time and effort) to the scientific community.
4. A timeline consistent with assessment objectives, the state of the underlying knowledge base, the resources available, and the needs of decision makers.
5. Engagement and commitment of interested and affected parties, with a transparent science-policy interface and effective communication throughout the process.
6. Strong leadership and an organizational structure in which responsibilities are well articulated.
7. Careful design of interdisciplinary efforts to ensure integration, with specific reference to the Assessment's purpose, users needs, and available resources.
8. Realistic and credible treatment of uncertainties.
9. An independent review process monitored by a balanced panel of review editors.
10. Maximizing the benefits of the Assessment by developing tools to support use of assessment results in decision making at differing geographic scales and decision levels.
11. Use of a nested assessment approach, when appropriate, using analysis of large-scale trends and identification of priority issues as the context for focused, smaller-scale impacts and response assessments at the regional or local level.

What is Already Underway: Federal Assessment Activities

Several Federal departments and agencies have ongoing or new activities related to climate change assessment. Efforts from three of those agencies were presented at the workshop and are highlighted here.

Department of the Interior (DOI)

Assessments are not new to DOI – in the past, USGS and DOI have led assessments related to topics such as minerals, commodities, water, and biodiversity. The primary focus of these efforts is not a single assessment, but rather creating a continuous and consistent process to look at how conditions have changed over time (*e.g.*, technologically recoverable *vs.* economically recoverable resources). The assessment process aims to be robust and policy relevant, but to avoid being policy prescriptive, by focusing on science. With climate change, the "rules" of assessment have changed – audiences are broader and the issues often exceed the scales and sector boundaries that have been used to frame past efforts.

Under Secretarial Order 3289 (fall, 2009), DOI is preparing to open eight new Climate Science Centers (CSCs) and 22 Landscape Conservation Cooperatives (LCCs). The CSCs will work at a regional level to bring together academic, state, and federal scientists and stakeholders and synthesize information to assess the effects and impacts of climate change. The regions will be Alaska, Northeast, Southeast, South Central, North Central, Northwest, Southwest, and Hawaiian Islands / Insular Properties, although there is not yet a designated process for how specific sites for the centers will be chosen. The CSCs will be a major source of science for the LCCs, which will in turn provide a science management interface with stakeholder communities – the place where science needed to inform decision making is delivered to the users. Although DOI will provide funding for the LCCs, the LCCs will be run by stakeholder-based boards of directors.

DOI and NOAA are working on a Memorandum of Understanding (MOU) to facilitate coordination and cooperation between the CSCs, LCCs, and the elements of NOAA's Regional Climate Centers and Climate Service, helping to ensure that the efforts of these entities will be complementary rather than competitive.

Environmental Protection Agency (EPA)

EPA's Global Change Research Program is an assessment-oriented program. Program activities are consistent with and closely coordinated with the U.S. Global Change Research Program; specific areas of emphasis include Air Quality, Water Quality/Aquatic Ecosystems, and Human Health. Across these program areas, the EPA Global Change Research Program addresses a wide variety of topics and methods for providing assessments and decision support products and is moving toward integrated decision support tools.

The EPA STAR Grant Program provides competitive, extramural funding to support high-quality research by the nation's leading scientists. Topics include global change effects on air pollution, water resources, ecosystems, and human health. The Climate Ready Estuaries program works to assess climate change vulnerabilities, create conceptual models for key indicators, develop and implement adaptation strategies, engage and educate stakeholders, and share the lessons learned with other coastal managers. Pilot projects exist in Massachusetts Bay and San Francisco Bay. (There is also a Climate Ready Utilities program).

The EPA's 20 Watershed Study conducts watershed modeling in order to understand sensitivity and vulnerability to climate and land use change, and is developing hydrologic and water quality change scenarios for 2040 to 2070.

National Oceanic and Atmospheric Administration (NOAA)

NOAA has supported a number of assessment-type activities over the years (e.g., Synthesis and Assessment Products within the Climate Change Science Program, State of the Climate reports, IPCC), but now recognizes that a new dimension must be added: ongoing engagement. Assessment services will be a central component of NOAA Climate Services that will be linked to the climate programs of other agencies into a National Climate Service, closely tied to USGCRP emerging plans and agency partners. Key sectoral strengths for climate service and assessment activities for NOAA are coasts and oceans; NOAA will build on existing partnerships and regional capacity across sectors and agencies (federal, state, and local).

Important goals for NOAA are to identify boundaries between NOAA's responsibilities and those of other partners and to create a sustainable, ongoing, and transparent process for assessment. Initial exploration into NOAA's Assessment Services will build on existing regional infrastructure (e.g., Regional Integrated Science and Assessment projects (RISAs), Regional Climate Centers (RCCs), State Climatologists, Cooperative Institutes, Sea Grant, external grants, and National Weather Service regions). Communication and education are critical and must be embedded in both the federal and the stakeholder side. To that end, a technical support unit will work with USGCRP to provide web resources, publishing, and other products. Other important aspects of NOAA's assessment services will include data access and transparency, downscaling of models, research, and other activities (e.g., attribution services).

What is Already Underway: Local, Regional, and International Assessment Activities

Local, regional and international assessment activities are already underway, and those involved in these assessment processes had several lessons to share and recommendations for the next National Assessment.

PlaNYC

The City of New York convened a panel on climate change to assess what climate change will likely mean for the city. The panel consisted of physical and social scientists and representatives from industry. In 2009, the panel provided a technical assessment as the basis of their climate change adaptation plan, named "PlaNYC," that is framed as a long-term sustainability plan. The report identified all of the potential risks to the City's critical infrastructure posed by climate change but also factored in air and water quality, and other environmental considerations. Representatives of city agencies, state agencies, and industry stakeholders, created an inventory of existing infrastructure that may be at-risk from the effects of climate change, and identified 300 adaptation strategies for managing climate risks.

California's Climate Action Team Reports

California's Climate Action Team is mandated by Governor Schwarzenegger to coordinate statewide efforts to implement global warming emission reduction programs and the state's Climate Adaptation Strategy. The state's Climate Action Team, comprised of technical representatives from state agencies, works with scientific community, nongovernmental organizations, and other partners to produce biennial science assessment reports that examine the impacts of climate change, evaluate the economic impacts, and develop strategies for adaptation. The assessment reports examine important interactions between eight important sectors with regard to climate impacts so that people can identify trade-offs. In the latest report, released in late 2009, climate impacts and emission reduction strategies were considered for each sector.

Union of Concerned Scientists Regional Assessments

The Union of Concerned Scientists has done a number of regionally focused assessments to help fill the gap after the First National Assessment. These reports relied on peer-reviewed scientific information from the IPCC Fourth Assessment Report and other scientific assessments. These reports identified a range of harmful and likely impacts on cities and ecosystems in a nine-state region.

During the development of these reports, the UCS placed co-equal emphasis on science and public outreach. Report authors across disciplines and geographies took media training. The UCS continued to engage stakeholders and the public beyond the report's release, and the message continued to spread and resonate through user communities. The UCS found windows of opportunity and "teachable moments." For example, during the debate about tailpipe regulation in California, the UCS released a report on the implications of different emissions scenarios for the state. The California Air Resources Board delivered a unanimous vote. This was not advocacy, but rather a strategically timed release of rigorous science.

Australia: Lessons on Assessment Based on the Down-Under Experience

Australia has tried several approaches to national assessments. The *Garnaut Review*, Australia's version of the Stern Report, translates climate projections into possible costs of impacts. Because the assessment provided little spatial relevance, it did not provide much information on adaptation that was useful operationally. A lesson from assessments in Australia is that they need to be "decision-centric," Such assessments can miss the fundamental point that the purpose of assessing adaptation options is to *develop options*; of adaptive capacity is to *build* solutions; and of vulnerability is to *reduce* risk. Australia has seen success with the Commonwealth Scientific and Industrial Research Organization (CSIRO), the country's national science agency, and its Energymark project. Energymark is a participatory

action research project that informs individuals about climate change and energy, and assists in changing behaviors for a sustainable future. The Energymark program works through a number of small community based networks. Each network group commits to a series of eight meetings to discuss energy and climate change based on balanced and authoritative information. After each meeting, the group convener sends a short summary of the key points raised and the CSIRO research team finds a scientist to answer the group's questions using the best science available. The program helps bring about and track large-scale behavioral change in Australian energy consumption patterns. Results so far have shown a mean reduction in carbon footprints by 27 percent and electricity consumption by 37.5 percent.

Australia's approach focuses on an ongoing process of assessment, rather than the product (a report). This dramatically shifts the emphasis on increasing adaptive capacity rather than on a static description of the status quo, and shifts the focus of assessment reports to a status report on the process rather than an end in themselves.

THE GARNAUT CLIMATE CHANGE REVIEW
Ross Garnaut

Cover used with permission from Cambridge University Press. Please see www.cambridge.org/us/9780521744447 for ordering details.

IPCC Fifth Assessment Report: An Update

The focus of the Intergovernmental Panel on Climate Change assessment report is shifting from "prove to me that climate change is real" to delivering the information needed to support stakeholders' decisions. The IPCC authors are increasingly aware that the climate issue needs to be framed as a problem of risk management. The generally accepted theory is that the public does not think in probabilistic terms but in fact, people make decisions under uncertainty every day and use probabilities in weighing their options. The IPCC assessments have also reached a level where they can discuss adaptation issues in addition to mitigation; the WGII outline includes several chapters on adaptation.

The IPCC is approaching the AR5 assessment as a single, integrated assessment. The broader social and economic narratives, themes of regional equity and generational justice, will accompany scenarios for the future. All of the working groups will cover cross cutting themes so that the dimensions of climate impacts and mitigation are dealt with in a comprehensive way. Each working group will address regional issues because that is where people are interfacing with climate system and making decisions. The regional chapters for Working Group Two will be more like a "one-stop shop" for assessing regional physical impacts and mitigation efforts.

Overall Recommendations from Other Ongoing Assessment Activities

Representatives from all of these assessment activities had many recommendations for the next National Assessment:

- If the goal of the National Assessment is to inform policy, it is vital that climate information users are connected, contributing to, and driving the Assessment process. The National Assessment could adopt a similar approach to Australia by establishing an ongoing, adaptive management program that is aimed to support multiple stakeholders. This program should be process-focused; projects should support solution-oriented discussions using excellent, rigorous science, and the combined knowledge of both scientists and user communities. The program should be rigorously monitored and evaluated so that if the United States were to adopt such an approach, the periodic assessment report to Congress could focus on the performance of adaptive management program. If the program is of value to stakeholders, the onus will be on Congress to stop it and suffer the political pain, rather than constantly trying to justify its own existence. Alternatively, if it is a standard "mini-IPCC" report, then the onus will be on the science and user communities to justify the report.

- In its 2009 form, the National Assessment describes the context for climate change but is not a tool for decision-making. A national assessment should attempt to relate climate change and frame it in a way that is familiar and understandable to stakeholders. Stakeholders make decisions every day under uncertainty using probabilities. They do not necessarily need more research or refined models; they just need to know the magnitude of the impact in terms that they can understand. For example, if New York is going to look like North Carolina by the middle of the century, then builders can assess what materials they use in North Carolina and start planning. The Assessment can also relate climate change to the seasonal and year-to-year climate variability issues we now face (snow storms, droughts, extreme weather, *etc.*).

- We need to coordinate federal science, and at the very least, coordinate information for use by decision-makers in sectors. Monitoring activities should continue to be a high priority because users need real-time data to make short-term decisions. However, assessments also inform long-term decisions.

- We need to foster a robust, public conversation on climate science. We need to take advantage of times when climate-related issues are receiving increased attention from the public because those are the "windows of opportunity" for effecting policies. An ongoing coordinated National Assessment effort should adopt an aggressive outreach strategy that extends beyond the release of the report. We missed this opportunity when the last National Assessment was released in 2009. One panelist compared it to writing a play and then only performing it once.

Key Messages Wrap-up: Approaches to the next National Climate Assessment

Workshop participants have been involved in a number of local, regional, national, and international assessment efforts and had much to offer on the subject of ways to approach the next round of the National Assessment. Building on conversations in previous sessions, the following themes emerged from the discussion.

Stakeholders are Critical

The number of people concerned about climate change grows every day, but we haven't necessarily done a good job of determining who the critical stakeholders are for the Assessment. The Assessment must quickly take on the task of defining its audience and planning for the ways that these stakeholders will be engaged. A process that encourages conversation and sharing of knowledge across all stakeholders will ultimately empower these stakeholders to make better decisions. Developing a robust stakeholder engagement process will take much time and effort, but the rich relationships that are built as a part of process are likely to be a major factor in the success of the Assessment overall.

Assessment is Both a Process and a Set of Products

The Assessment must be a living process in order to best identify and be responsive to the questions and needs of stakeholders. Regular reports developed as a part of this process are useful in establishing baselines that help everyone understand what is happening already and what is likely to happen in the future. Such reports also serve as a mechanism to crystallize our thinking.

Themes within the Assessment

There is no one "right" way to slice the Assessment into regions or sectors. Many of the impacts of climate change cut across regions or must be considered in the context of interactions between sectors. Thus it will be important to design a process that is flexible enough to allow for sharing across whatever bins are ultimately chosen for doing the work. The following themes can serve as potential central organizing concepts.

- Adaptation and Mitigation. This new round of assessment must acknowledge the close connections between science, adaptation, and mitigation. We must move beyond questions of whether climate change is happening; the questions now must focus on an "end to end" understanding of climate change impacts and response strategies. Readjusting the focus in this way will open the door to a much larger set of stakeholders and partners, many of whom will bring perspectives that have not been considered in previous rounds of assessment. This expanded set of issues will require reformulating our ideas about "experts" and governance structures for the Assessment.

- Sustainability. While the GCRA calls for a periodic report on "global change," we really must use the Assessment process to think more inclusively about sustainability of human and natural systems, especially in the face of increased variability in weather and extreme events. The Assessment should be situated within a decision-focused, comprehensive sustainability framework so that lessons and insights can be more immediately connected to the needs of stakeholders.

- Regions. The impacts of climate change are ultimately recognized and dealt with at local and regional scales, and thus large portions of the Assessment must be developed primarily by stakeholders and experts drawn from each region. If large portions of the Assessment process are seen as valuable and are owned at a variety of levels (local to national), it is more likely that the overall process will be less vulnerable to

changes in institutions and administrations and more responsive to the needs of stakeholders.

Sharing the Messages

It is essential to build into the process capabilities for sharing insights across regions and sectors in ways that are accessible to a broad range of stakeholders. This means that we must quickly develop a strategy for communicating about the products of the Assessment. This strategy should include plans for communicating about the Assessment process itself as well as how to match products with users, any education or training required for product dissemination and use, and how to engage the necessary translators and integrators in communicating about the Assessment. There are already many specialists in "translation" or "integration" across the boundaries of science, policy, and decision making; the task now is to identify where these specialists currently reside within Federal, academic, NGO, or private sector institutions and to find ways to engage their knowledge and skills as a part of the Assessment process. Furthermore, the Assessment process should find ways to encourage additional training and development of new translators and integrators.

Coordinating Across Federal Efforts

The National Assessment process has an important role to play in helping establish a process and set of products that is well-aligned with other ongoing activities at the local, state, Federal, and international levels for both the practitioners and users of assessments. It can support other important climate activities, such as climate services and adaptation efforts. Standing up an assessment process that is responsive to the needs of the stakeholders will require drawing on the capabilities of all the federal agencies, including those not currently considered a part of the USGCRP. Because this effort spans the government, the ultimate champions for the effort must include the Office of Science and Technology Policy and the Council on Environmental Quality. Reinvigorating the Committee on Environment and Natural Resources can also assist in providing interagency coordination, especially if the subcommittees' focus areas are appropriately constructed (*i.e.*, not too broad). Planning for the Assessment will also require the federal government to face the task of defining relationships between the USGCRP, agency efforts related to climate science and services (*e.g.*, NOAA Climate Services, DOI Climate Science Centers), and interagency efforts related to adaptation and mitigation. Presenting these efforts in a coordinated fashion will benefit both the agencies and task forces that are leading them and the broader public as it seeks to engage in learning about and making decisions related to climate change.

Coordinating Across Assessment Efforts

The number of efforts related to climate change is quickly growing, as cities, states, international bodies, NGOs, and private industry all attempt to craft assessment and planning efforts that will best meet their needs. In many cases these efforts draw upon the same participants, quickly leading to assessment fatigue as the finite time and human resources are exhausted. The National Assessment process must consider how to better coordinate across these efforts and how these might feed into each other rather than compete; a process of particular concern is the Intergovernmental Panel on Climate Change Fifth Assessment Report.

Shared National and Regional Leadership

Some portions of the Assessment require central coordination, while others can only be accomplished successfully by people working in individual regions or sectors. Stakeholders are more likely to trust and engage with the Assessment process if there is clear leadership from within their region. Prior to the First National Assessment, there was little capacity for assessing and responding to the impacts of climate change. Now, several local and regional governments have surpassed federal capabilities and have implemented their own processes to assess the impacts of climate change and develop plans for adaptation and mitigation; such capabilities should be harnessed via a national system that facilitates sharing between regions and which can assist regions that are less advanced in coming up to speed. Leadership at the regional level should be housed at a neutral or trustworthy institution, such as a university (or consortium of universities) or a national laboratory. Selecting the host sites may still be fraught with difficulties (*e.g.*, competition between institutions, controlling overhead charges, *etc.*), but the benefits of having this local connection are tremendous.

Adequate Resources

As discussed above under the heading "Coordinating Across Federal Efforts," the Assessment effort will span multiple agencies; therefore, the resources for the Assessment must come from across federal government. Furthermore, aligning regional and sectoral assessment efforts will require coordination – and resources for that coordination – from the federal

level. There are multiple ways to accomplish this task – including through the shared budget mechanism currently used to support activities within USGCRP; providing a directed appropriation to one agency, with the understanding that the agency is coordinating and conducting the Assessment on behalf of and in cooperation with all of the agencies; or relying on individual agencies to conduct pieces of the Assessment with minimal budgetary coordination between them. Using the distributed cost mechanism, in which each agency "has skin in the game," is one way to ensure that the Assessment is seen as an interagency priority; however, the cost of the Assessment activity could quickly overwhelm other USGCRP priorities and the current mix of agencies and programs counted in the distributed cost algorithm may not be appropriate for calculating contributions for the National Assessment. Alternatively, providing an appropriation to one agency may have the advantage of simplifying responsibility and reporting mechanisms for the effort. It is also important that a portion of the Assessment budget can be quickly accessed for novel and high-impact activities; even setting aside 5 percent of the annual expected contributions will allow the Assessment to be much more nimble in addressing the science, information, and capacity needs identified as a part of the Assessment process.

Building an Enduring Assessment Structure

Drawing on the discussions described in the above "Framing the Assessment" and "Understanding the Alternatives" sections, participants offered a number of suggestions and ways to move forward on building an enduring assessment structure. The suggested activities can be grouped under a number of action items, described below. These are not presented in a specific priority or time sequence order; many of these actions must begin now and be carried out in parallel, while others will naturally follow on as the Assessment process takes shape.

Start Now

We cannot afford to lose any time in working toward an operational National Assessment. It will require quite a bit of effort to get many pieces of the Assessment up and running; starting immediately on this tasks is essential in order to meet the 2013 deadline, especially if we might begin delivering some products ahead of this deadline. As the various pieces of the Assessment come into focus, we must also engage with Congress and with stakeholders to ensure that the process being laid out will be responsive to statutory requirements and stakeholder needs.

Establish Oversight and Governance Structures

Both Agencies and non-Federal stakeholders should be involved in the oversight and governance of the National Assessment. Federal partners in USGCRP are responsible for ensuring that the Assessment takes place, and thus there will need to be an interagency mechanism aimed at identifying and coordinating financial and human resources for the Assessment and overseeing the implementation of the Assessment; this may take the form of a new interagency committee, or it may be added to the scope of an existing committee such as the USGCRP Principals. However, there must also be an overarching governance structure that reaches beyond the federal government, especially if the Assessment will rely heavily on a regionally-distributed and co-owned model of work. This "board of governors" might be modeled after that of a 501c3 organization, should have an officially-chartered role, and include strong representation from federal agencies, regions, sectors, and grassroots interests. Likely this "board of governors" would have to be set up to be in compliance with the FACA, thus work should begin quickly so that it is in place before the Assessment is too far along. The board may resemble the National Assessment Synthesis Team from the First National Assessment in some ways (e.g., provide input back to Agencies about how well the Assessment is progressing, play a role in reporting to and engaging external groups), although having an exact copy of the NAST would likely not be appropriate.

Define the Assessment

Having a clear definition of what the Assessment is intended to be – including its vision, mission, goals, and general plan of action – is essential before the process moves much further. The Assessment can be both a process and a product, but we need to define up front how we will accomplish this integration in a way that is responsive to both the statutory requirements for a periodic "Assessment" and the needs of stakeholders for more regular discussion and decision support. Different groups of stakeholders may have widely divergent view of what is meant by "National Assessment," and not all expectations for what the Assessment will deliver may be met. It will be vital to manage expectations from the outset through early and ongoing stakeholder engagement.

Identify and Engage Stakeholders

There are multiple audiences for the process and products of the Assessment, but we have engaged them unevenly in previous rounds of assessment. Now we need to draw up a blueprint for moving forward in a more stakeholder-driven, or at least stakeholder-relevant, fashion. We need to identify key audiences and determine how best to bring them into the process and we need to build access points for new stakeholders to join the process as it progresses. We must make a commitment to engage with stakeholders in the places where they live and work; this will be time-consuming and will require staff to be "on the ground" in regions to better understand who the various players in the area are, what the public discourse on climate change is (or isn't), and what the important issues are.

Identify and Prioritize Stakeholders' Needs

We have to consult with stakeholders in order to ascertain their needs and questions, then prioritize our activities based on our own risk-based criteria. We should also consider how to document needs and questions as a part of the Assessment, so that results can be tied to specific drivers. One way to engage stakeholders and tease out specific needs and questions could be through the use of small, community-based networks similar to those used as a part of Australia's Energymark program, which convene a set of stakeholders for a series of conversations. Some of the outputs from an assessment of stakeholder needs can also be used to inform the development of climate services.

Mapping Capacity and Capabilities

There are already assessment-type activities, data clearinghouses, and other related activities at local, state, regional, national, and international levels that could feed into a National Assessment. However, we often are unaware of the broad range of activities and resources because they are not well networked, and thus we cannot help others discover these existing resources. Therefore, an early step in the Assessment process should be to create a map of where various capacities and capabilities reside – both the data sources and the human knowledge needed to do the work of assessment. We can also use this map as a basis for gap analysis – understanding where additional support is needed to develop capacity and capabilities that will be essential to the Assessment process.

Aligning with and Building onto Existing Activities

The capacity and capability map will help lead us to existing activities that should be incorporated into the National Assessment or which should be linked to the Assessment process. At the local to regional level, such activities include city climate plans (*e.g.*, Chicago, New York, Seattle) and state adaptation assessments (*e.g.*, California). At the national level there are also a number of existing and emerging activities, including DOI's Climate Science Centers, NOAA's Climate Service, and the CEQ/NOAA/OSTP Adaptation Task Force, that should work in cooperation with the National Assessment; more work is needed to bound the responsibilities of these entities and describe how they will work together on issues of common interest. Finally, efforts such as the National Research Council's "America's Climate Choices" study has much to say about many of the issues that might be covered by the National Assessment – rather than repeating the work of these panels, we will need to build up from their findings to tackle new questions.

Moving from Vulnerability to Resilience

There has never been a national assessment of vulnerability, but this seems like it would be a good place to start. By focusing on the various dimensions of vulnerability (ecological, social, economic, *etc.*), we would move away from the tendency to start with the physical climate and could instead begin to build an assessment that identifies the most vulnerable areas, specific risks (both from climate and other stressors), and ultimately describe ways that communities are taking action to or preparing to make natural and human systems more resilient.

The Nested Matrix Approach

It will be impossible to create an assessment that addresses all climate change impacts and responses at all levels of society. Instead, we should consider implementing the "nested matrix" approach described above, in which we identify a number of priority issues and then carry out case studies or other smaller-scale impacts and response assessments at local to regional and sectoral levels. Such an approach would require sustaining a baseline system of observations and monitoring, which in turn would help identify areas in which changes are of particular concern, and thus are targets for more focused study. This approach is also more flexible funding-wise, as the number of cases can be expanded or contracted in response to funding constraints.

Data, Observations, and Trusted Sources

We should maintain a focus on real-time observations and seek to put current observations into an historical focus. As a part of the capacity and capability mapping described above, we should take the time to educate ourselves about the sources of data across the federal government. However, the federal government is not the only source of data; for example, emergency management agencies have much to data contribute from both socio-economic and natural environments. With the many sources of data flowing into the Assessment process, we will need coordinated data management – we need to know where to find information and how to combine data streams from different sources. In addition to data streams, there are many other types of input that will require careful management, including findings from other assessment processes and reports from a variety of stakeholder groups. One issue that meeting participants highlighted was the need to find ways to "whiten" the grey literature; although it is clear that we will need to draw on a broader source literature than what has been used in the past, many of these sources have not been produced using the peer review process that is standard in scientific communities. One way that this "whitening" could begin almost immediately is to sponsor "mini-Dahlem" conferences, in which those who have produced the grey literature come together and work together to produce peer-reviewed papers based on synthesis of underlying "grey literature" pieces.

A Strategy for Communications

Communication is a critical component of the Assessment and must be embedded from the start of the process. Therefore, we must develop a communications strategy quickly, and this strategy must promote communication throughout the Assessment process. We already have a lot of information that is already ready to go out and can quickly be passed along to a broad community of stakeholders and partners, including the "Highlights" brochures from the 2009 report *Global Climate Change Impacts in the United States* and a variety of materials from agencies. We also have a number of new communications tools at our disposal, including social media and webinars, which can be used both to promote relevant products and to engage stakeholders.

Outcomes-Based Measures of Success

Evaluation will be a key portion of the Assessment process – and must take place throughout, so that we can adjust the process before it becomes irrelevant. The National Assessment cannot succeed if it is only done to "check a box" – satisfying perhaps the letter of the GCRA, but not the spirit of the Assessment requirement. The metrics chosen to evaluate the Assessment process should be outcomes-focused, but not so plentiful that the number of expected outcomes completely overwhelms the process. One way to ensure that the measures of success are relevant is to define them in cooperation with the various audiences for the Assessment – including Congress, federal agencies, state and local governments, and other stakeholders. Having these audiences involved at the start will also help to manage their expectations throughout the process and to make certain that the Assessment will be trusted and used. We may be able to learn from activities such as the NOAA RISAs, which have several years experience in tracking how decision making processes have been affected by science contributions.

Next Steps

Participants generally agreed that the initial "straw man" outline for mission, goals, principles, and timeline is appropriate; however, it is still unclear whether near-term meetings in support of developing a strategic plan should be focused primarily on identifying issues of concern in various regions, or whether there should be a focus on developing components of the Assessment itself. These "process components" are important in building permanent assessment capacity, *e.g.*, guidelines for risk and vulnerability assessment, new approaches to cost-benefit analysis (risk of acting *vs.* not acting), approaches to prioritizing issues of concern, capacity building for connecting climate science with decision processes, designing communication and education strategies, and cyber-infrastructure for a national clearinghouse for adaptation and mitigation activities. In addition, we anticipate that the National Academies will soon be asked to engage in the process to review either process or products or both.

High-priority issues include deciding on a timeline for delivering the National Assessment; establishing an interagency working group to guide the Assessment process; and assembling an inventory of existing national, regional, state, and sectoral assessment activities and products. There is a need to set up process workshops that help build sectoral, regional and other parts of the Assessment.

Appendix A: Agenda

Wednesday, February 24

4:00 – 4:30 pm	**OSTP vision and charge to the group; introduction to the strategic planning process** T. Karl (Introductions), Shere Abbott (invited), Kathy Jacobs
4:30 – 5:00	**Panel discussion on mission, vision, principles for the National Climate Assessment** J. Melillo (Chair), Panelists: Ed Miles, Virginia Burkett, Brad Udall, David Behar
5:00 – 6:00	**Open discussion of mission, vision, principles**
6:00 – 6:30	**Reception**
6:30	**Dinner** Chris Field, Co-Chair, IPCC Working Group II, "An International Perspective on Climate Assessment"

Thursday, February 25

7:00 – 8:00 am	**Continental breakfast**
8:00 – 8:45	**Report on agency assessment activities** D. Wuebbles (Chair), Panelists: Tom Armstrong (DOI), Anne Grambsch (EPA), Eileen Shea (NOAA)
8:45 – 9:30	**Report on other assessment activities** T. Janetos (Chair), Panelists: John Andrew (California DWR), Mark Howden (CSIRO Australia), Adam Freed (New York City), Peter Frumhoff (Union of Concerned Scientists), Chris Field (IPCC)
9:30 – 9:45	**Break**
9:45 – 10:30	**Alternative approaches to structuring and governing the Assessment** Rosina Bierbaum (Chair), Panelists: Jim Mahoney, Jim Buizer, Eileen Shea, Mike MacCracken, Tom Armstrong
10:30 – 11:45	**Breakout groups: Building an enduring assessment structure, components of the assessment report (chapters, regions, scenarios, connections with IPCC, data access, *etc.*), for the National Climate Assessment** Facilitators: D. Ferguson, A. Grambsch, K. Averyt Rapporteurs: N. Engle, E. Cloyd, A. Waple
11:45 – 12:45	**Lunch** Rosina Bierbaum, University of Michigan, "Whither the National Assessment?"

12:45 – 2:00	**Breakout groups: Assessment process and governance, timeline, staffing alternatives, partnerships, measures of success** Facilitators: F. Laurier, J. Foster, K. Wood Rapporteurs: L. Carter, J. Austin, J. Samenow
2:00 – 2:30	**Break -- Rapporteurs summarize findings**
2:30 – 3:30	**Report back to plenary; summary and discussion of outcomes**
3:30 – 4:00	**Discussion of next steps**
4:00	**Adjourn**

Appendix B: Participant List

Donald E. Anderson
NOAA Climate Program Office
1315 East-West Hwy, SSMC3, Rm. 12-108
Silver Spring, MD 20910
Tel: 301-734-1222
Fax: 301-713-0518
Email: don.anderson@noaa.gov

John Andrew
Assistant Deputy Director
California Department of Water Resources
1416 Ninth St.
P.O. Box 942836
Sacramento, CA 94236-0001
Tel: 916-651-9657
Fax:
Email: jandrew@water.ca.gov

Thomas R. Armstrong
Senior Advisor for Climate Change
Office of the Deputy Secretary
U.S. Department of the Interior
1849 C St., NW
Washington, DC 20240
Tel: 202-208-6713; Cell - 703-304-0229
Fax: 202-208-1873
Email: tarmstrong@usgs.gov

Jennifer Austin
NOAA Communications & External Affairs
Washington, DC
Tel: 202-482-5757; Cell: 202-302-9047
Fax:
Email: jennifer.austin@noaa.gov

Kristen B. Averyt
Deputy Director
NOAA-CIRES, Western Water Assessment
University of Colorado at Boulder
NOAA Earth System Research Laboratory
325 Broadway R/PSD
Boulder, CO 80305-3328
Tel: 303-497-4344; Cell: 303-827-1059
Fax:
Email: kristen.averyt@noaa.gov

John Balbus
Director
NIEHS
P.O. Box 12233
111 TW Alexander Dr.
MD: B2-01, Room B240
Durham, NC 27709
Tel: 919-541-3201
Fax:
Email: john.balbus@nih.gov

John Bates
Remote Sensing and Applications Division
NOAA National Climatic Data Center
151 Patton Ave., Rm. 120
Asheville, NC 28801
Tel: 828-271-4378
Fax: 828-271-4328
Email: john.j.bates@noaa.gov

David Behar
Climate Program Director, San Francisco PUC
Staff Chair, Water Utility Climate Alliance
1145 Market St., 4th Fl.
San Francisco, CA 94103
Tel: 415-554-3221
Fax:
Email: dbehar@sfwater.org

Rosina Bierbaum
World Development Report 2010
World Bank
1818 H Street, NW
Washington, DC 20433
Tel: 202-473-1000
Fax:
Email: rbierbaum@worldbank.org

Rona Birnbaum
Chief, Climate Science & Impacts Branch
Climate Change Division
U.S. Environmental Protection Agency
1200 Pennsylvania Ave., NW
Washington, DC 20460
Tel: 202-343-9076
Fax:
Email: birnbaum.rona@epa.gov

Maria Blair
Deputy Associate Director
for Climate Change Adaptation
White House Council on Environmental Quality (CEQ)
Executive Office of the President
722 Jackson Place
Washington, DC 20503
Tel: 202-456-1475
Fax: 202-456-6546
Email: mblair@ceq.eop.gov

Otis Brown
Rosenstiel School of Marine and Atmospheric Sciences
University of Miami
4600 Rickenbacker Causeway
Miami, FL 33149-1031
Tel: 305-421-4000
Fax: 305-421-4711
Email: obrown@miami.edu

James L. Buizer
Executive Director
Strategic Institutional Advancement
and Policy Advisor to the President
Arizona State University
P.O. Box 877705
Tempe, AZ 85287-7705
Tel: 480-965-6515
Fax: 480-965-0865
Email: buizer@asu.edu

Lawrence Buja
RAL
NCAR
P.O. Box 3000
Boulder, CO 80307
Tel: 303-497-1330
Fax:
Email: southern@ucar.edu

Virginia Burkett
U.S. Geological Survey
540 N. Courthouse St.
Many, LA 71449
Tel: 318-256-5628
Fax:
Email: virginia_burkett@usgs.gov

Lynne M. Carter
Director, Adaptation Network
Assoc. Director, RISA, LSU
Assoc. Director, Sustainability Agenda
Louisiana State University
E-333 Howe-Russell
Baton Rouge, LA 70803
Tel: 401-527-6058; Cell: 401-527-6058
Fax:
Email: lynne@srcc.lsu.edu

Emily T. Cloyd
Carbon & Ecosystem Support Program Specialist
U.S. Global Change Research Program1717 Pennsyl-
vania Ave., NW, Ste. 250
Washington, DC 20006
Tel: 202-419-3484; Cell: 202-286-9642
Fax: 202-223-3065
Email: ecloyd@usgcrp.gov

Heidi M. Cullen
Climate Central
One Palmer Square
Princeton, NJ 08540
Tel: 609-986-1986
Fax:
Email: hcullen@climatecentral.org

Nathan Engle
School of Natural Resources and Environment
University of Michigan
2209 W. Byron, #3
Chicago, IL 60618
Tel: 484-695-6185
Fax:
Email: nengle@umich.edu

Jack D. Fellows
Vice President for Corporate Affairs
Director, UCAR Community Programs
University Corporation for Atmospheric Research
P.O. Box 3000-FL4
Boulder, CO 80307-3000
Tel: 303-497-8655
Fax: 303-497-8638
Email: jfellows@ucar.edu

Daniel Ferguson
Program Manager
Climate Assessment for the Southwest (CLIMAS)
Institute for the Environment
University of Arizona
P.O. Box 210156
Tucson, AZ 85719
Tel: 520-622-8918
Fax: 520-792-8795
Email: dferg@email.arizona.edu

Chris Field
Director, Department of Global Ecology
Carnegie Institution of Washington
Stanford University
260 Panama St.
Stanford, CA 94305
Tel: 650-462-1047 x201; Cell: 650-823-5326
Fax: 650-462-5968
Email: cfield@ciw.edu

Paul Fleming
Manager
Climate and Sustainability Group
Seattle Public Utilities
700 5th Ave. Suite 4900
PO Box 34018
Seattle, WA 98124-4018
Tel: 206-684-7626
Fax:
Email: paul.fleming@seattle.gov

Joshua Foster
Center for Clean Air Policy
750 First Street, NE, Ste. 940
Washington, DC 20002
Tel: 202-408-9260
Fax: 202-408-8896
Email: jfoster@ccap.org

Guido Franco
California Energy Commission
1516 Ninth Street, MS-29
Sacramento, CA 95814-5512
Tel: 916-654-3940
Fax:
Email: gfranco@energy.state.ca.us

Adam Freed
Deputy Director
Mayor's Office of Long-Term Planning & Sustainability
City of New York
New York, NY
Tel: 212-788-8843
Fax: 212-788-1558
Email: afreed@cityhall.nyc.gov

Peter Frumhoff
National Headquarters
Union of Concerned Scientists
2 Brattle Square
Cambridge, MA 02238
Tel: 617-301-8027
Fax: 617-864-9405
Email: pfrumhoff@ucsusa.org

Ned Gardiner
Climate Visualization Project Manager
NOAA Climate Program Office
NOAA National Climatic Data Center
151 Patton Ave., Rm. 557C
Asheville, NC 28801-5006
Tel:
Fax:
Email: ned.gardiner@noaa.gov

Anne Grambsch
Global Change Research Program,
National Center for Env. Assessment
U.S. Environmental Protection Agency
Two Potomac Yard (North Bldg)
2733 South Crystal Dr., Room N-7631
Arlington, VA 22202
Tel: 703-347-8521
Fax: 703-347-8694
Email: grambsch.anne@epamail.epa.gov

Steve Hipskind
Division Chief, Earth Science Division
NASA Ames Research Center
MS 245-4
Moffett Field, CA 94035-1000
Tel: 650-604-5076; Cell: 650-279-1570
Fax: 650-604-3625
Email: steve.hipskind@noaa.gov

Leonard P. Hirsch
Smithsonian Institution
1100 Jefferson Drive SW #3123
PO Box 3701
Q-3123 MRC 705
Washington, DC 20013-7012
Tel: 202-633-4788
Fax: 202-312-2888
Email: lph@si.edu

Mark Howden
Sustainable Ecosystems
CSIRO
Gungahlin Homestead
Bellenden Street
Crace, ACT 2911
AUSTRALIA
Tel: (61) 2-6242-1679
Fax:
Email: mark.howden@csiro.au

Tom Iseman
Program Director for Water Policy
Western Governors' Association
1600 Broadway, Ste. 1700
Denver, CO 80202
Tel: 303-623-9378
Fax: 303-534-7309
Email: tiseman@westgov.org

Brian Jackson
Project Coordinator
Joint Office for Science Support
University Corporation for Atmospheric Research
P.O. Box 3000 - FL4, Rm 2334
Boulder, CO 80307-3000
Tel: 303-497-8663
Fax: 303-497-8633
Email: bjackson@ucar.edu

Katharine L. Jacobs
Assistant Director for Assessments and Adaptation
White House Office of Science and Technology Policy
U.S. Global Change Research Program Office
1717 Pennsylvania Ave, NW, Ste. 250
Washington, DC 20006
Tel:
Fax:
Email: jacobsk@email.arizona.edu

Anthony C. Janetos
Director
Joint Global Change Research Institute
Pacific Northwest National Laboratory/
University of Maryland
5825 University Research Ct., Ste. 3500
Baltimore, MD 20740
Tel: 301-314-7843
Fax: 301-314-6719
Email: Anthony.janetos@pnl.gov

Alexa K. Jay
Research Associate, Climate Science Watch
Government Accountability Project
1612 K Street, NW Suite 1100
Washington, DC 20006
Tel: 206-849-5060
Fax:
Email: alexakjay@gmail.com

Thomas R. Karl
Director, National Climatic Data Center
Lead, NOAA Climate Services
NOAA National Climatic Data Center
Veach-Baley Federal Building
151 Patton Ave., Rm. 557C
Asheville, NC 28801-5006
Tel: 828-271-4476
Fax: 828-271-4246
Email: thomas.r.karl@noaa.gov

Jill Karsten
Program Director for Education and Diversity
Directorate for Geosciences
National Science Foundation
4201 Wilson Blvd.
Arlington, VA 22230
Tel: 703-292-8500
Fax:
Email: jkarsten@nsf.gov

Jack Kaye
Acting Director
US Global Change Research Program
1717 Pennsylvania Avenue, Suite 250
Washington, DC 20006
Tel: 202-358-0757
Fax:
Email: jack.kaye@nasa.gov

Caitlyn Kennedy
Science Writer
NOAA Climate Program Office
1315 East-West Highway, SSMC-3
Silver Spring, MD 20910
Tel: 301-734-1219; Cell: 301-706-0285
Email: caitlyn.kennedy@noaa.gov

Timothy Killeen
Geosciences Assistant Director
National Science Foundation
4201 Wislon Bouldevard
Arlington, VA 22230
Tel: 703-292-8500
Fax: 703-292-9042
Email: tkilleen@nsf.gov

Chester J. Koblinsky
NOAA Climate Goal Lead
Director, Climate Program Office
NOAA Climate Program Office
1315 E. West Highway, SSMC3
Rm. 12837 North
Silver Spring, MD 20910
Tel: 301-734-1233
Fax: 301-713-0515
Email: chester.j.koblinsky@noaa.gov

Fabien J.G. Laurier
NSTC Subcommittee on Global Change Research
U.S. Global Change Research Program
1717 Pennsylvania Ave, NW, Ste. 250
Washington, DC 20006
Tel: 202-419-3481; Cell: 202-288-2879
Fax:
Email: flaurier@usgcrp.gov

Linda Lawson
Director, Office of Safety, Energy and Environment
U.S. Department of Transportation
1200 New Jersey Avenue, SE
Washington, DC 20590
Tel: 202-366-4416; Cell: 202-366-4835
Fax: 202-366-0263
Email: linda.lawson@dot.gov

Stuart Levenbach
Office of Management and Budget
Executive Office of the President
725 17th St. NW, Room 9215
Washington, DC 20503
Tel: 202-395-3915
Fax: 202-395-1150
Email: stuart_levenbach@omb.eop.gov
Charles Lin
Environment Canada
4905 Dufferin Street
Toronto, ON
CANADA
Tel:
Fax:
Email: Charles.lin@ec.gc.ca

Diana Liverman
Institute of the Environment
The University of Arizona
Tucson, AZ 85721
Tel: 520-388-0190
Fax:
Email: liverman@u.arizona.edu

Amy Luers
Senior Environmental Science Manager
Google.org
900 Alta Ave.
Mountain View, CA 94043
Tel: 415-736-1013
Fax:
Email: amyluers@google.com

Jeffrey C. Luvall
Global Hydrology and Climate Center
NASA -NSSTC
320 Sparkman Drive
Huntsville, AL 35805
Tel: 256-961-7886
Fax: 256-961-7788
Email: jluvall@nasa.gov

Michael MacCracken
Chief Scientist for Climate Change Programs
Climate Institute
900 17th St., Ste. 700 (with Heinz Center)
Washington, DC 20006
Tel: 202-552-4723
Fax: 202-737-6410
Email: mmaccrac@comcast.net

James R. Mahoney
Environmental Consultant
18482 Lanier Island Square
Leesburg, VA 20176
Tel: 703-777-6333
Fax:
Email: mahoneyenv@aol.com

Sabrina McCormick
Fellow, American Association for the
Advancement of Science
U.S. Environmental Protection Agency
George Washington University
US EPA (8601-P)
1200 Pennsylvania Ave., NW
Washington, DC 20460
Tel: 215-898-5456
Fax:
Email: sabrina.mccormick@gmail.com

Chad McNutt
National Integrated Drought Information System
(NIDIS) Program Office
NOAA Earth System Research Laboratory
325 Broadway (R/PSD)
Boulder, CO 80305-3328
Tel: 303-497-5481
Fax: 303-497-7013
Email: chad.mcnutt@noaa.gov

Linda Mearns
Environmental and Societal Impacts Group
National Center for Atmospheric Research
P.O. Box 3000 - ML
Boulder, CO 80307
Tel: 303-497-8124
Fax: 303-497-8125
Email: lindam@ucar.edu

Jerry Melillo
Director
Marine Biological Laboratory
7 MBL St.
Woods Hole, MA 02543
Tel: 508-289-7494
Fax: 508-457-1548
Email: jmelillo@mbl.edu

Edward L. Miles
Co-Director, Center for Science in the Earth System
Director, Climate Impacts Group
JISAO, Dept. of Atmospheric Science
University of Washington
Box 355672
Seattle, WA 98195-5672
Tel: 206-685-1837 or 206-616-5348
Fax: 206-543-1417 or 206-616-5775
Email: edmiles@u.washington.edu

Christopher Miller
Program Manager, Climate Change Data and Detec-
tion
NOAA Climate Program Office
1100 Wayne Avenue, 12th Floor
Silver Spring, MD 20910
Tel: 301-734-1241
Fax: 301-713-0517
Email: Christopher.d.miller@noaa.gov

Kathryn Moran
Office of Science and Technology Policy
Executive Office of the President
New Executive Office Building
725 17th St., NW, Ste. 7217 (5th floor)
Washington, DC 20038
Tel:
Fax:
Email: kathryn_moran@ostp.eop.gov

Richard H. Moss
Senior Staff Research Scientist
Joint Global Change Research Institute
University of Maryland
5825 University Research Ct., Ste. 3500
College Park, MD 20740
Tel: 301-314-6711; Cell: 202-468-5441
Fax:
Email: rhm@pnl.gov

Frank Niepold
Climate Science Literacy Coordinator
UCAR/NOAA Climate Program Office
1315 East-West Hwy., SSMC3
Rm. 12727 North
Silver Spring, MD 20910
Tel: 301-734-1244; Cell: 240-429-0038
Fax: 301-713-0518
Email: frank.niepold@noaa.gov

Roger Pulwarty
Director, National Integrated Drought Information Syst
em (NIDIS) Program Office
NOAA Earth System Research Laboratory
325 Broadway (R/PSD)
Boulder, CO 80305
Tel: 303-497-4425
Fax: 303-497-7013
Email: roger.pulwarty@noaa.gov

V. Ramaswamy
Director, National Integrated Drought Information
System (NIDIS) Program Office
NOAA Earth System Research Laboratory
325 Broadway (R/PSD)
Boulder, CO 80305
Tel: 609-452-6510
Fax: 609-987-5063
Email: v.ramaswamy@noaa.gov

Kelly T. Redmond
Regional Climatologist/Deputy Director
Western Regional Climate Center
Desert Research Institute
2215 Raggio Pkwy.
Reno, NV 89512-1095
Tel: 775-674-7011
Fax: 775-674-7016
Email: krwrcc@dri.edu

Paul J. Runci
Joint Global Change Research Institute
Pacific Northwest National Laboratory
University of Maryland
5825 University Research Ct., Ste. 3500
Baltimore, MD 20740
Tel: 301-314-7843
Fax: 301-314-6719
Email: paul.runci@pnl.gov

Jason Samenow
Climate Science & Impacts Branch
Climate Change Division
U.S. Environmental Protection Agency
1200 Pennsylvania Ave. NW
Washington, DC 20460
Tel:
Fax:
Email: samenow.jason@epamail.epa.gov

Don Scavia
Graham Family Professor and Director
Graham Environmental Sustainability Institute
Professor, School of Nat. Res. & Environment
Professor, Civil and Env. Engineering
University of Michigan
Ann Arbor, MI 48109-1041
Tel: 734-615-4860
Fax:
Email: scavia@umich.edu

Eileen Shea
Chief, Climate Services Division
National Climatic Data Center, NOAA/NESDIS
Veach-Baley Federal Building, Room 468
151 Patton Avenue
Asheville, NC 28801-5001
Tel: 828-271-4384
Fax: 828-271-4876
Email: eileen.shea@noaa.gov

A.J. Singletary
U.S. Department of Transportation
1200 New Jersey Avenue, SE
Washington, DC 20590
Tel: 202-366-0360
Fax: 202-366-0263
Email: arthur.singletary@dot.gov

Brooke Stewart
Department of Atmospheric Sciences
University of Illinois
105 S. Gregory Street
Urbana, IL 61801
Tel: 217-333-9604
Fax:
Email: stewar14@atmos.uiuc.edu

Bradley H. Udall
Director
Western Water Assessment
University of Colorado at Boulder
NOAA Earth System Research Laboratory
325 Broadway R/PSD
Boulder, CO 80305-3328
Tel: 303-497-4573
Fax: 303-497-6449
Email: Bradley.udall@colorado.edu

Dan Walker
Chief, Climate Assessments and Services Division
NOAA Climate Program Office
1315 East-West Highway, SSMC-3
Silver Spring, MD 20910
Tel: 301-734-1212
Fax: 301-713-0518
Email: daniel.walker@noaa.gov

Margaret Walsh
Climate Change Program Office
U.S. Department of Agriculture
1400 Independence Ave., SW
Washington, DC 20250
Tel: 202-720-9978
Fax: 202-401-1176
Email: mwalsh@oce.usda.gov

Anne M. Waple
NOAA National Climate Data Center
Veach-Baley Federal Building
151 Patton Ave.
Asheville, NC 28801
Tel: 828-257-3000
Fax:
Email: anne.waple@noaa.gov

Thomas Wilbanks
ORNL Corporate Fellow
Group Leader, MultiScale Energy-Environmental Systems, Environmental Sciences Division
Oak Ridge National Laboratory
Bethel Valley Road, Building 1505, Room 356A
Oak Ridge, TN 37831-6038
Tel: 865-574-5515
Fax: 865-576-2943
Email: wilbankstj@ornl.gov

Karen Wood
Internal and Web Communications Officer
Office of Communications
U.S. Geological Survey
119 National Center
Reston, VA 20192
Tel: 703-648-4447
Fax: 703-648-4466
Email: kwood@usgs.gov

Donald J. Wuebbles
The Harry E. Preble Professor of Atmospheric Sciences
School of Earth, Society, and Environment
Department of Atmospheric Sciences
University of Illinois
105 S. Gregory St
Urbana, IL 61801-3070
Tel: 217-244-1568
Fax: 217-244-4393
Email: wuebbles@uiuc.edu

Appendix C:

Next Generation Scenarios for Assessment

Traditionally, model-based scenarios used in climate change research have been developed using a sequential process that is time-consuming, and causes delays and inconsistencies across research areas. In the February 11, 2010 issue of *Nature*, an international team of climate scientists detailed a new approach for developing the next generation of scenarios for climate change research and assessment.[1]

The next set of models will include, for the first time, tightly linked analyses of greenhouse gas emissions, projections of the Earth's climate, impacts of climate change, and human decision-making. Climate change researchers established a new coordinated parallel process for developing scenarios. The process starts with four scenarios that are defined by how much of the sun's energy the atmosphere retains. Multiple factors affect this, including greenhouse gas accumulation, the presence of atmospheric particles, and land use. The scientists called each of these futures a "representative concentration pathway," or RCP. Many groups of scientists will use the RCPs in climate models to project changes in a range of climate conditions including temperature, precipitation and extreme events, taking into account recent climate observations and new information about climate system processes.

A diverse range of socioeconomic scenarios could produce any particular climate future or RCP. The concept presents opportunities for research and assessment across many disciplines. Integrated assessment modelers can research how different human futures increase or decrease emissions of pollutants and activities that cause climate change. This type of modeling will focus on population and economic growth, the evolution of technologies, and other factors such as governmental policies. Other teams of researchers will then use the results of these climate and socio-economic studies in a wide range of research on the potential effects of climate change on natural resources, human health, coastal infrastructure, ecosystems and other sectors.

This approach will influence the next international scientific assessment undertaken by the Intergovernmental Panel on Climate Change (IPCC). It will provide the framework for informing studies that evaluate adaptation needs and strategies, explore mitigation options, and improve understanding of potentially large feedbacks in the climate system. Additional steps are needed to realize the full potential of the process, but the open-ended nature of the process and a new sequence for research adaptation promises to speed up the exchange of information between scientists and provide decision-makers with better tools to deal with a shifting climate.

---

[1] Moss, R.H. *et al.*, 2010. The next generation of scenarios for climate change research and assessment. *Nature* 463: 747-756.